BOB'S BURGERS

GRAND RE-OPENING

MAD LIBS®

by Billy Merrell

Mad Libs

An Imprint of Penguin Rand~~om~~

MAD LIBS
Penguin Young Readers Group
An Imprint of Penguin Random House LLC

Mad Libs format copyright © 2018 by Penguin Random House LLC. All rights reserved.

Concept created by Roger Price & Leonard Stern

™ & © 2018 Twentieth Century Fox Film Corporation. All Rights Reserved.

Published by Mad Libs,
an imprint of Penguin Random House LLC,
345 Hudson Street, New York, New York 10014.
Printed in the USA.

ISBN 9781524787349
3 5 7 9 10 8 6 4

MAD LIBS® is a game for people who don't like games! It can be played by one, two, three, four, or forty.

• RIDICULOUSLY SIMPLE DIRECTIONS

In this tablet you will find stories containing blank spaces where words are left out. One player, the READER, selects one of these stories. The READER does not tell anyone what the story is about. Instead, he/she asks the other players, the WRITERS, to give him/her words. These words are used to fill in the blank spaces in the story.

• TO PLAY

The READER asks each WRITER in turn to call out a word—an adjective or a noun or whatever the space calls for—and uses them to fill in the blank spaces in the story. The result is a MAD LIBS® game.

When the READER then reads the completed MAD LIBS® game to the other players, they will discover that they have written a story that is fantastic, screamingly funny, shocking, silly, crazy, or just plain dumb—depending upon which words each WRITER called out.

• EXAMPLE (*Before* and *After*)

"_____ !" he said _____
    EXCLAMATION   ADVERB

as he jumped into his convertible _____ and
                        NOUN

drove off with his _____ wife.
             ADJECTIVE

"**OUCH** !" he said **STUPIDLY**
    EXCLAMATION   ADVERB

as he jumped into his convertible **CAT** and
                        NOUN

drove off with his **BRAVE** wife.
             ADJECTIVE

In case you have forgotten what adjectives, adverbs, nouns, and verbs are, here is a quick review:

An ADJECTIVE describes something or somebody. *Lumpy*, *soft*, *ugly*, *messy*, and *short* are adjectives.

An ADVERB tells how something is done. It modifies a verb and usually ends in "ly." *Modestly*, *stupidly*, *greedily*, and *carefully* are adverbs.

A NOUN is the name of a person, place, or thing. *Sidewalk*, *umbrella*, *bridle*, *bathtub*, and *nose* are nouns.

A VERB is an action word. *Run*, *pitch*, *jump*, and *swim* are verbs. Put the verbs in past tense if the directions say PAST TENSE. *Ran*, *pitched*, *jumped*, and *swam* are verbs in the past tense.

When we ask for A PLACE, we mean any sort of place: a country or city (*Spain*, *Cleveland*) or a room (*bathroom*, *kitchen*).

An EXCLAMATION or SILLY WORD is any sort of funny sound, gasp, grunt, or outcry, like *Wow!*, *Ouch!*, *Whomp!*, *Ick!*, and *Gadzooks!*

When we ask for specific words, like a NUMBER, a COLOR, an ANIMAL, or a PART OF THE BODY, we mean a word that is one of those things, like *seven*, *blue*, *horse*, or *head*.

When we ask for a PLURAL, it means more than one. For example, *cat* pluralized is *cats*.

MAD LIBS® is fun to play with friends, but you can also play it by yourself! To begin with, DO NOT look at the story on the page below. Fill in the blanks on this page with the words called for. Then, using the words you have selected, fill in the blank spaces in the story.

Now you've created your own hilarious MAD LIBS® game!

BURGER JUICE

NUMBER _____

SILLY WORD _____

ADJECTIVE _____

TYPE OF FOOD _____

NUMBER _____

TYPE OF LIQUID _____

PERSON IN ROOM _____

SILLY WORD _____

ADJECTIVE _____

PART OF THE BODY _____

ADJECTIVE _____

COLOR _____

PART OF THE BODY _____

CELEBRITY (MALE) _____

ADJECTIVE _____

COLOR _____

PART OF THE BODY _____

VERB _____

BURGER JUICE

Want to lose _____ pounds faster than you can say
                  NUMBER

_____? Try one of Linda's simple and _____
SILLY WORD   ADJECTIVE

burger-in-a-glass recipes:

_____ **À La Mode:** In a blender, combine _____
TYPE OF FOOD   NUMBER

bananas, two cups of _____, and one large scoop of
                     TYPE OF LIQUID

_____ brand ice cream. For a little extra _____,
PERSON IN ROOM   SILLY WORD

add a splash of _____-brew coffee. Yum!
                ADJECTIVE

Bob's _____ **Feta-ish:** In a juicer, process two
          PART OF THE BODY

_____ stalks of celery, three _____ beets, and a/an
ADJECTIVE   COLOR

_____-ful of parsley. Garnish with feta cheese!
PART OF THE BODY

_____'s **Moustache:** Blend one _____
CELEBRITY (MALE)   ADJECTIVE

avocado with a pint of fresh _____ juice. (The foam sticks to
                             COLOR

your upper _____ when you _____ it—hence
           PART OF THE BODY   VERB

the name!)

MAD LIBS® is fun to play with friends, but you can also play it by yourself! To begin with, DO NOT look at the story on the page below. Fill in the blanks on this page with the words called for. Then, using the words you have selected, fill in the blank spaces in the story.

Now you've created your own hilarious MAD LIBS® game!

FLASH MOB

PERSON IN ROOM _____

A PLACE _____

NUMBER _____

TYPE OF FOOD _____

A PLACE _____

ADJECTIVE _____

PLURAL NOUN _____

ADJECTIVE _____

TYPE OF FOOD _____

LETTER OF THE ALPHABET _____

COLOR _____

NOUN _____

ARTICLE OF CLOTHING _____

PERSON IN ROOM (FEMALE) _____

VERB ENDING IN "ING" _____

NUMBER _____

FLASH MOB

When Mr. _____'s assistant accidentally included the
PERSON IN ROOM

address to Bob's _____ on a party invite, _____
A PLACE   NUMBER

of Ocean Avenue's top elites showed up expecting free _____.
TYPE OF FOOD

"The _____ promotion must be working!" Bob told Linda,
A PLACE

excited to see _____ customers. But when the
ADJECTIVE

_____ started to complain, he knew something was
PLURAL NOUN

_____. "I most certainly specified _____ on the
ADJECTIVE   TYPE OF FOOD

RSV-_____, not *beef*," said a woman in a/an
LETTER OF THE ALPHABET

_____ dress and _____ earrings. "And where is
COLOR   NOUN

the caviar?" Felix Fischoeder arrived, wearing a/an _____
ARTICLE OF CLOTHING

over his face—which he removed when he realized where he was.

"This isn't the Fischoeder Fling! Aunt _____, let's
PERSON IN ROOM (FEMALE)

get out of here!" Felix began immediately _____ guests
VERB ENDING IN "ING"

away. "You forgot your check!" Bob yelled after him. "Someone owes

me _____ dollars!"
NUMBER

MAD LIBS® is fun to play with friends, but you can also play it by yourself! To begin with, DO NOT look at the story on the page below. Fill in the blanks on this page with the words called for. Then, using the words you have selected, fill in the blank spaces in the story.

Now you've created your own hilarious MAD LIBS® game!

LOUISE, P.I.

NOUN _____

COLOR _____

NOUN _____

VERB _____

TYPE OF LIQUID _____

CELEBRITY (FEMALE) _____

PLURAL NOUN _____

NUMBER _____

SILLY WORD _____

COLOR _____

VERB ENDING IN "ING" _____

PART OF THE BODY _____

ANIMAL _____

EXCLAMATION _____

VERB _____

PLURAL NOUN _____

VERB ENDING IN "ING" _____

ADJECTIVE _____

LOUISE, P.I.

When the storefront next to the Belchers' _____ closed
                                                    NOUN

again, Louise decided to investigate. She ducked under the

_____ police tape warning: _____ *Scene! Do Not*
COLOR   NOUN

_____! Once inside, the _____ ran cold in her
VERB   TYPE OF LIQUID

veins. There were photographs of _____ pinned to the
                                   CELEBRITY (FEMALE)

wall, along with newspaper _____ about her. On
                            PLURAL NOUN

_____ of the photos, _____ was written in
NUMBER   SILLY WORD

_____ marker. There was a/an _____ bag
COLOR   VERB ENDING IN "ING"

on the floor, along with a/an _____-guard and—stranger
                               PART OF THE BODY

still—a teddy _____. "_____," Louise said,
               ANIMAL   EXCLAMATION

reaching out to _____ it. As she did, she heard a man's
                 VERB

_____ behind her! "What are you doing
PLURAL NOUN

_____ around my set?!" It was Randy, video camera in
VERB ENDING IN "ING"

hand. And from the look on his face, he wasn't _____.
                                                ADJECTIVE

MAD LIBS® is fun to play with friends, but you can also play it by yourself! To begin with, DO NOT look at the story on the page below. Fill in the blanks on this page with the words called for. Then, using the words you have selected, fill in the blank spaces in the story.

Now you've created your own hilarious MAD LIBS® game!

TROUBLE IN TINA-TOWN

NOUN _____

VERB ENDING IN "ING" _____

VERB _____

VERB _____

TYPE OF FOOD _____

NOUN _____

VERB ENDING IN "ING" _____

ADJECTIVE _____

VERB ENDING IN "ING" _____

NOUN _____

ADJECTIVE _____

A PLACE _____

CELEBRITY (FEMALE) _____

PART OF THE BODY _____

PLURAL NOUN _____

TROUBLE IN TINA-TOWN

This is the worst _____ of my life! I have been
NOUN

_____ for over an hour, and I don't think I'll ever
VERB ENDING IN "ING"

_____! I'm used to Jimmy Jr. ignoring me, but today he
VERB

didn't _____ at me *once*—not even when I gave him the
VERB

_____ I was saving for dessert. What a/an _____!
TYPE OF FOOD   NOUN

He ate it without _____ me or anything! I wanted to
VERB ENDING IN "ING"

smack the crumbs right off his _____ face! (Louise, if you're
ADJECTIVE

_____ this, STOP RIGHT NOW or I'll tell our
VERB ENDING IN "ING"

_____!) It wasn't all _____, though. In the
NOUN   ADJECTIVE

afternoon, I followed Jimmy Jr. to (the) _____ and caught
A PLACE

him dancing alone to _____ songs. I love the way his
CELEBRITY (FEMALE)

_____ moves to the music. I could hear him humming the
PART OF THE BODY

_____ to my favorite song!
PLURAL NOUN

MAD LIBS® is fun to play with friends, but you can also play it by yourself! To begin with, DO NOT look at the story on the page below. Fill in the blanks on this page with the words called for. Then, using the words you have selected, fill in the blank spaces in the story.

Now you've created your own hilarious MAD LIBS® game!

GENE'S PRESERVES

ADVERB _____

TYPE OF CONTAINER _____

ADJECTIVE _____

PLURAL NOUN _____

ADJECTIVE _____

ARTICLE OF CLOTHING _____

VERB _____

VERB _____

TYPE OF LIQUID _____

PLURAL NOUN _____

ADJECTIVE _____

TYPE OF FOOD _____

PLURAL NOUN _____

PART OF THE BODY _____

ADJECTIVE _____

NOUN _____

ADJECTIVE _____

GENE'S PRESERVES

Here are Gene's Dos and Don'ts for _____ catching a fart in
                                      ADVERB

a/an _____:
     TYPE OF CONTAINER

DO: Go somewhere _____! Some _____ may
                      ADJECTIVE   PLURAL NOUN

consider it _____ to drop your _____ in
            ADJECTIVE   ARTICLE OF CLOTHING

public. Plus, you don't want to under-_____ the element of
                                       VERB

surprise!

DO: _____ what you eat! Like a fine _____,
        VERB   TYPE OF LIQUID

flatulence contains a multitude of _____! _____
                                   PLURAL NOUN   ADJECTIVE

notes of _____, for example, or an undercurrent of
         TYPE OF FOOD

_____. Trust your _____!
PLURAL NOUN   PART OF THE BODY

DO: Form a/an _____ seal. The less outside _____
                  ADJECTIVE   NOUN

that gets in, the better.

DON'T: Hold back! The secret to a/an _____ specimen is
                                         ADJECTIVE

confidence!

MAD LIBS® is fun to play with friends, but you can also play it by yourself! To begin with, DO NOT look at the story on the page below. Fill in the blanks on this page with the words called for. Then, using the words you have selected, fill in the blank spaces in the story.

Now you've created your own hilarious MAD LIBS® game!

ZEKE ATTACK

PERSON IN ROOM (MALE) _____

VERB _____

ADJECTIVE _____

PLURAL NOUN _____

PLURAL NOUN _____

ADJECTIVE _____

PART OF THE BODY _____

ANIMAL _____

ADJECTIVE _____

PART OF THE BODY _____

NOUN _____

VERB _____

NUMBER _____

VERB ENDING IN "ING" _____

ADJECTIVE _____

ZEKE ATTACK

Zeke's rules for wrestling matches with _____ Pesto Jr.:

PERSON IN ROOM (MALE)

1. Scrimmages can start at any time, so be ready to _____

VERB

without warning!

2. _____ fighters fight No _____ Barred!

ADJECTIVE   PLURAL NOUN

Only _____ worry about getting _____.

PLURAL NOUN   ADJECTIVE

So scissor holds, _____-locks, and _____

PART OF THE BODY   ANIMAL

hugs are all _____ game! (Especially if I have the

ADJECTIVE

upper _____.)

PART OF THE BODY

3. NO DANCING! The middle of a wrestling _____ is

NOUN

no time to _____ a rug!

VERB

4. Winner receives _____ points and infinite

NUMBER

_____ rights.

VERB ENDING IN "ING"

Hope you're _____, cause I'm gonna getcha!

ADJECTIVE

MAD LIBS® is fun to play with friends, but you can also play it by yourself! To begin with, DO NOT look at the story on the page below. Fill in the blanks on this page with the words called for. Then, using the words you have selected, fill in the blank spaces in the story.

Now you've created your own hilarious MAD LIBS® game!

TWIN PEEKS

NOUN _____

A PLACE _____

NOUN _____

PLURAL NOUN _____

NUMBER _____

OCCUPATION _____

VERB _____

ADJECTIVE _____

PLURAL NOUN _____

PART OF THE BODY _____

VERB ENDING IN "ING" _____

TYPE OF FOOD (PLURAL) _____

OCCUPATION _____

VERB ENDING IN "ING" _____

PLURAL NOUN _____

VERB _____

VERB _____

TWIN PEEKS

Andy and Ollie were the only witnesses of a/an _____ that
NOUN

broke out at Jimmy Pesto's _____, but when asked who
A PLACE

threw the first _____, the twins gave conflicting
NOUN

_____. According to Ollie, it was _____ -for-
PLURAL NOUN NUMBER

one pizza night, and the _____ Jimmy Jr. had snuck off to
OCCUPATION

_____ in the back. Ollie heard a/an _____ crash,
VERB ADJECTIVE

and when he looked up, his father's wall of _____ had
PLURAL NOUN

toppled on its own. According to Andy, though, it was Pastafarian

night. Bob had ripped the Rasta hat off Jimmy Pesto's

_____, and the men were _____ about
PART OF THE BODY VERB ENDING IN "ING"

the recipe for Pesto's Bestos _____. The
TYPE OF FOOD (PLURAL)

_____ responding to the incident couldn't get Andy and
OCCUPATION

Ollie to stop _____ once they were pulled apart.
VERB ENDING IN "ING"

When the _____ were reunited, they hugged and refused
PLURAL NOUN

to _____ further. "Let's never _____ again."
VERB VERB

MAD LIBS® is fun to play with friends, but you can also play it by yourself! To begin with, DO NOT look at the story on the page below. Fill in the blanks on this page with the words called for. Then, using the words you have selected, fill in the blank spaces in the story.

Now you've created your own hilarious MAD LIBS® game!

WHICH BELCHER KID ARE YOU?

ADJECTIVE _____

FIRST NAME (MALE) _____

VERB _____

NOUN _____

PLURAL NOUN _____

A PLACE _____

ADJECTIVE _____

NOUN _____

COLOR _____

ANIMAL _____

PLURAL NOUN _____

ADJECTIVE _____

PART OF THE BODY _____

NOUN _____

NOUN _____

ADJECTIVE _____

ADVERB _____

FIRST NAME (FEMALE) _____

WHICH BELCHER KID
ARE YOU?

1. In your _____ time, you are most likely to:
   ADJECTIVE

   (a) pine for your friend _____, (b) _____
   FIRST NAME (MALE)   VERB

   music on your electric _____, (c) practice picking
                          NOUN

   _____
   PLURAL NOUN

2. You wouldn't dare leave (the) _____ without:
                                  A PLACE

   (a) your _____-framed eyeglasses, (b) your electric
            ADJECTIVE

   _____, (c) your _____ _____ hat
   NOUN   COLOR   ANIMAL

3. Your _____ ground you for no _____
        PLURAL NOUN   ADJECTIVE

   reason. You: (a) pour your _____ out about it in
                              PART OF THE BODY

   your _____, (b) compose a/an _____ about
        NOUN   NOUN

   _____ parenting, (c) escape _____!
   ADJECTIVE   ADVERB

If you answered mostly a, you're Tina; mostly b, you're Gene; mostly c,

you're _____!
       FIRST NAME (FEMALE)

MAD LIBS® is fun to play with friends, but you can also play it by yourself! To begin with, DO NOT look at the story on the page below. Fill in the blanks on this page with the words called for. Then, using the words you have selected, fill in the blank spaces in the story.

Now you've created your own hilarious MAD LIBS® game!

INTERVIEW WITH A NEIGH-SAYER

NUMBER _____

ADJECTIVE _____

NOUN _____

COLOR _____

CELEBRITY (MALE) _____

ANIMAL _____

SILLY WORD _____

NUMBER _____

ADJECTIVE _____

LAST NAME _____

TYPE OF FOOD _____

ARTICLE OF CLOTHING (PLURAL) _____

VERB _____

ADJECTIVE _____

NOUN _____

ANIMAL _____

INTERVIEW WITH
A NEIGH-SAYER

Tina: I have here the self-proclaimed "number _____ fan"
NUMBER

of *The Equestranauts*. So, Bronconius, what makes you think you're

such a/an _____ fan?
  ADJECTIVE

Bronconius: I prefer the term *Equesticle*. Would a run-of-

the-_____ "fan" own a/an _____-plated Minnie
      NOUN   COLOR

once owned by _____? I think not.
              CELEBRITY (MALE)

T: Well, let's pretend for a moment you weren't top _____.
                                                        ANIMAL

Who would be?

B: Interesting. Well, _____-puddle might be second.
                          SILLY WORD

He does have _____ of the _____ Edition
              NUMBER   ADJECTIVE

_____ ponies, a prized Sea-_____ doll, and more
  LAST NAME   TYPE OF FOOD

Equestranaut _____ than anyone else I know.
              ARTICLE OF CLOTHING (PLURAL)

T: Ahem. Does anyone else _____ to mind? Perhaps a young
                              VERB

and _____ writer of _____-fiction?
    ADJECTIVE   NOUN

B: You, an *Equesticle*? Little girl, you're not even wearing a/an

_____ costume.
  ANIMAL

MAD LIBS® is fun to play with friends, but you can also play it by yourself! To begin with, DO NOT look at the story on the page below. Fill in the blanks on this page with the words called for. Then, using the words you have selected, fill in the blank spaces in the story.

Now you've created your own hilarious MAD LIBS® game!

HOW TO BE BURGERBOSS

NOUN _____

TYPE OF FOOD _____

VERB ENDING IN "ING" _____

VERB _____

NOUN _____

ANIMAL _____

TYPE OF LIQUID _____

ADJECTIVE _____

OCCUPATION _____

NOUN _____

VERB _____

PLURAL NOUN _____

PLURAL NOUN _____

VERB (PAST TENSE) _____

ADJECTIVE _____

VERB _____

HOW TO BE BURGERBOSS

Bob's tutorial from Darryl, a/an _____ game enthusiast:
<u>NOUN</u>

Like many classic games, _____-boss is a side-_____
<u>TYPE OF FOOD</u> <u>VERB ENDING IN "ING"</u>

puzzle platform type game. The objective is to _____
<u>VERB</u>

through each _____ and defeat anthropomorphic
<u>NOUN</u>

villains, such as _____ legs, _____ bottles,
<u>ANIMAL</u> <u>TYPE OF LIQUID</u>

and _____ peppers. The player is a/an _____ whose
<u>ADJECTIVE</u> <u>OCCUPATION</u>

only weapon is a/an _____ cleaver. He must
<u>NOUN</u>

_____ across the rooftops of _____ or down
<u>VERB</u> <u>PLURAL NOUN</u>

in the _____ below the city, fighting enemies along
<u>PLURAL NOUN</u>

the way. As with any endeavor, practice makes perfect. Don't

be _____ by the game's music! It's loud and _____
<u>VERB (PAST TENSE)</u> <u>ADJECTIVE</u>

by design. My advice: Become one with the character—and then

_____ for your life!
<u>VERB</u>

MAD LIBS® is fun to play with friends, but you can also play it by yourself! To begin with, DO NOT look at the story on the page below. Fill in the blanks on this page with the words called for. Then, using the words you have selected, fill in the blank spaces in the story.

Now you've created your own hilarious MAD LIBS® game!

WAGSTAFF SCHOOL NEWS

NOUN _____

LETTER OF THE ALPHABET _____

VERB ENDING IN "ING" _____

TYPE OF FOOD (PLURAL) _____

NOUN _____

NOUN _____

SILLY WORD _____

VERB _____

NUMBER _____

CELEBRITY _____

ADJECTIVE _____

VERB _____

VERB ENDING IN "ING" _____

NUMBER _____

NOUN _____

ADJECTIVE _____

PLURAL NOUN _____

WAGSTAFF SCHOOL NEWS

Filling in for anchor-_____ Tammy Larsen, this is Linda
                        NOUN

Belcher, a concerned _____-TA member. There is
                      LETTER OF THE ALPHABET

_____ news at this hour! The _____
VERB ENDING IN "ING"   TYPE OF FOOD (PLURAL)

Colleen Caviello donated for this year's _____ sale are *not*
                                            NOUN

homemade. And I can prove it! I found a/an _____-Mart
                                              NOUN

receipt while I was unpacking Colleen's so-called _____
                                                    SILLY WORD

Cookies. And _____ right here! She paid _____
              VERB   NUMBER

dollars and forty-two cents for _____'s famous
                                   CELEBRITY

_____ Chocolate _____-doodles. Now she's
ADJECTIVE   VERB

_____ them off as her own, and charging
VERB ENDING IN "ING"

_____ dollars more? Well, not on my _____, Colleen!
NUMBER   NOUN

What else haven't you been _____ about? Tell us. I think the
                            ADJECTIVE

teachers and _____ of Wagstaff deserve an answer.
              PLURAL NOUN

MAD LIBS® is fun to play with friends, but you can also play it by yourself! To begin with, DO NOT look at the story on the page below. Fill in the blanks on this page with the words called for. Then, using the words you have selected, fill in the blank spaces in the story.

Now you've created your own hilarious MAD LIBS® game!

GENE FOR A DAY

ADJECTIVE _____

NOUN _____

ADVERB _____

TYPE OF FOOD _____

NOUN _____

CELEBRITY _____

NOUN _____

NOUN _____

NOUN _____

FIRST NAME (FEMALE) _____

PLURAL NOUN _____

ADJECTIVE _____

NUMBER _____

PART OF THE BODY _____

VERB (PAST TENSE) _____

ADJECTIVE _____

TYPE OF FOOD (PLURAL) _____

PART OF THE BODY (PLURAL) _____

GENE FOR A DAY

After a prank gone _____ led to a minor injury at the grill,
          ADJECTIVE

Gene insisted on being pampered by Linda. First, Gene had her fetch

_____ cubes and aloe for his _____ noticeable
     NOUN   ADVERB

burns. Then he asked Linda to bring him _____ and milk,
                                            TYPE OF FOOD

run him a/an _____ bath, and read to him in her best
                 NOUN

_____ voice, the way she did when he was a/an
   CELEBRITY

_____. It was the hot _____ massage that was
     NOUN   NOUN

a/an _____ too far for Linda. She agreed reluctantly, but it was
        NOUN

_____ who returned! And with a bucket of steaming
FIRST NAME (FEMALE)

_____! "_____ enough for you?" she cackled,
 PLURAL NOUN   ADJECTIVE

placing them _____ at a time on Gene's lower
                 NUMBER

_____. Gene _____, but quickly calmed
PART OF THE BODY   VERB (PAST TENSE)

back down. "Yes, actually. They're the _____ temperature.
                                          ADJECTIVE

Thank you. And more sliced _____, please!"
                            TYPE OF FOOD (PLURAL)

Gene added. "For my _____!"
                     PART OF THE BODY (PLURAL)

MAD LIBS® is fun to play with friends, but you can also play it by yourself! To begin with, DO NOT look at the story on the page below. Fill in the blanks on this page with the words called for. Then, using the words you have selected, fill in the blank spaces in the story.

Now you've created your own hilarious MAD LIBS® game!

LETTER FROM CAMP

NOUN _____

ANIMAL _____

NOUN _____

ADJECTIVE _____

ANIMAL _____

NUMBER _____

VERB ENDING IN "ING" _____

ADJECTIVE _____

COLOR _____

VERB ENDING IN "ING" _____

ADVERB _____

PART OF THE BODY _____

ARTICLE OF CLOTHING _____

VERB (PAST TENSE) _____

PART OF THE BODY _____

PLURAL NOUN _____

NOUN _____

LETTER FROM CAMP

Dear Mom and Dad,

I'm having the _____ of my life at _____ camp!
               NOUN   ANIMAL

I impressed the _____ counselor with my _____
               NOUN   ADJECTIVE

knowledge of horses. Seems those issues of _____ *Illustrated*
                                      ANIMAL

finally paid off! I can't believe it's only _____ days until our
                               NUMBER

_____ exhibition! I've been assigned to a/an
VERB ENDING IN "ING"

_____ stallion named Plops. He's old and _____,
ADJECTIVE   COLOR

and he's always _____—hence his name! But that's
                VERB ENDING IN "ING"

okay. I still love him _____. Plops and I are getting along
                   ADVERB

much better. He hasn't stepped on my _____, knocked
                               PART OF THE BODY

my _____ off with his tail, or _____
   ARTICLE OF CLOTHING   VERB (PAST TENSE)

my hair since the first day. And he's only peed on my

_____-pack twice! Thank you again for making my
PART OF THE BODY

_____ come true!
PLURAL NOUN

Your loving _____, Tina
              NOUN

MAD LIBS® is fun to play with friends, but you can also play it by yourself! To begin with, DO NOT look at the story on the page below. Fill in the blanks on this page with the words called for. Then, using the words you have selected, fill in the blank spaces in the story.

Now you've created your own hilarious MAD LIBS® game!

ADVICE FOR MR. FROND

NOUN _____

PART OF THE BODY _____

ADJECTIVE _____

VERB _____

LETTER OF THE ALPHABET _____

NOUN _____

FIRST NAME (MALE) _____

NOUN _____

PART OF THE BODY _____

ADVERB _____

ARTICLE OF CLOTHING _____

VERB _____

OCCUPATION _____

SAME OCCUPATION _____

VERB _____

NOUN _____

ADJECTIVE _____

ADVICE FOR MR. FROND

During detention with Mr. Frond, Louise gives her _____
NOUN

counselor the following advice:

- No one likes a tattle-_____. Congratulations, you
  PART OF THE BODY

  can tell _____ from wrong! Doesn't mean you have
  ADJECTIVE

  to _____ it all the time. What are you, part of the
  VERB

  _____-GB?
  LETTER OF THE ALPHABET

- Prioritize! Other students at Wagstaff need your _____
  NOUN

  more than I do! I hear Pocket Sized _____ doesn't
  FIRST NAME (MALE)

  even know what _____ he's in! Surely, that's a problem.
  NOUN

- Time for a/an _____-cut? How do I say this
  PART OF THE BODY

  _____ . . . Do you own a mirror? Knit yourself a new
  ADVERB

  _____, at least. Sheesh!
  ARTICLE OF CLOTHING

- Don't _____ so hard! This whole good
  VERB

  _____ / bad _____ shtick reeks of effort.
  OCCUPATION   SAME OCCUPATION

  Just _____ back and ride the _____. When
  VERB   NOUN

  it comes to "guidance," a little goes a/an _____ way.
  ADJECTIVE

MAD LIBS® is fun to play with friends, but you can also play it by yourself! To begin with, DO NOT look at the story on the page below. Fill in the blanks on this page with the words called for. Then, using the words you have selected, fill in the blank spaces in the story.

Now you've created your own hilarious MAD LIBS® game!

TEDDY'S HOME BREW

PLURAL NOUN _____

NOUN _____

VERB _____

NOUN _____

LAST NAME _____

OCCUPATION _____

NOUN _____

ADJECTIVE _____

A PLACE _____

TYPE OF LIQUID _____

PART OF THE BODY _____

ADJECTIVE _____

ADJECTIVE _____

PLURAL NOUN _____

VERB (PAST TENSE) _____

TYPE OF LIQUID _____

PART OF THE BODY _____

FIRST NAME (MALE) _____

TEDDY'S HOME BREW

When the Belchers woke to loud _____ coming from
                                    PLURAL NOUN

Mort's _____ Home, Bob went next door to _____
          NOUN   VERB

on the place. He found Teddy in the _____-room,
                                         NOUN

surrounded by beakers and _____ burners. He looked like a
                              LAST NAME

mad _____ conducting a/an _____. "I was
       OCCUPATION   NOUN

_____, Bobby," Teddy explained. "I'm supposed to be
   ADJECTIVE

_____-sitting. But I figured I'd make some home-brewed
   A PLACE

_____ for Mort to take my _____ off how
   TYPE OF LIQUID   PART OF THE BODY

spooky this place is." "Are you sure it's _____ to use his
                                              ADJECTIVE

equipment?" Bob asked. "Who knows how many _____
                                                ADJECTIVE

bodies and toxic _____ this stuff has touched."
                     PLURAL NOUN

"I _____ it all with _____," Teddy said
     VERB (PAST TENSE)   TYPE OF LIQUID

defensively. But the idea made his _____ turn. "Maybe
                                      PART OF THE BODY

let's not tell _____," Teddy added. "In case he's squeamish."
                FIRST NAME (MALE)

MAD LIBS® is fun to play with friends, but you can also play it by yourself! To begin with, DO NOT look at the story on the page below. Fill in the blanks on this page with the words called for. Then, using the words you have selected, fill in the blank spaces in the story.

Now you've created your own hilarious MAD LIBS® game!

SCAREDY-CATS

ADJECTIVE _____

VERB _____

OCCUPATION _____

ADJECTIVE _____

SAME OCCUPATION _____

PART OF THE BODY _____

ANIMAL (PLURAL) _____

PART OF THE BODY (PLURAL) _____

VERB ENDING IN "ING" _____

VERB ENDING IN "ING" _____

NUMBER _____

PERSON IN ROOM (MALE) _____

ANIMAL _____

COLOR _____

ANIMAL _____

NOUN _____

ANIMAL (PLURAL) _____

TYPE OF LIQUID _____

SCAREDY-CATS

Though the Belchers *seem* calm, _____, and collected, they
                                          ADJECTIVE

aren't entirely un-_____-able. Here is a list of Belcher family
                        VERB

phobias:

- Otherwise fearless, Louise is afraid of her _____.
                                                      OCCUPATION

  She had a/an _____ cavity but *still* wouldn't let her
                     ADJECTIVE

  _____ pull the _____.
    SAME OCCUPATION   PART OF THE BODY

- Gene is afraid of slithering _____, allegedly because
                                    ANIMAL (PLURAL)

  they lack _____ and legs.
              PART OF THE BODY (PLURAL)

- Tina has had nightmares about _____ zombies
                                      VERB ENDING IN "ING"

  ever since Bob let her watch *Night of the* _____
                                                  VERB ENDING IN "ING"

  Dead when she was _____ years old.
                          NUMBER

- Linda's worst fear is her son, _____, turning
                                      PERSON IN ROOM (MALE)

  into a/an _____. Or, possibly, running out of
                  ANIMAL

  _____ wine.
        COLOR

But the biggest "scaredy-_____" of all is Bob. Though his
                              ANIMAL

greatest _____ is failure, he's also afraid of being attacked by
            NOUN

_____ and faints at the sight of his own _____!
ANIMAL (PLURAL)   TYPE OF LIQUID

MAD LIBS® is fun to play with friends, but you can also play it by yourself! To begin with, DO NOT look at the story on the page below. Fill in the blanks on this page with the words called for. Then, using the words you have selected, fill in the blank spaces in the story.

Now you've created your own hilarious MAD LIBS® game!

FEELING SAUCY

NUMBER _____

NOUN _____

NOUN _____

LAST NAME _____

TYPE OF LIQUID _____

NUMBER _____

NOUN _____

PLURAL NOUN _____

ADJECTIVE _____

VERB _____

NOUN _____

PART OF THE BODY _____

ADJECTIVE _____

PART OF THE BODY _____

VERB ENDING IN "ING" _____

VERB _____

A PLACE _____

FEELING SAUCY

To celebrate the _____-year anniversary of their
                         NUMBER

_____, Bob surprised Linda with a romantic _____
     NOUN   NOUN

of the Day. It incorporated Chateau _____, Linda's favorite
                                        LAST NAME

brand of _____. (Though perhaps too much.) It took Bob
         TYPE OF LIQUID

_____ tries to perfect the recipe, and by the time he
   NUMBER

unlocked the _____ to the restaurant, he had accidentally
                 NOUN

drunk half a bottle, and was three _____ to the wind.
                                        PLURAL NOUN

"_____ anniversary!" Bob told Linda with a hiccup. "You
   ADJECTIVE

have to _____ this sauce!" He held a/an _____-ful
           VERB   NOUN

of it inches from Linda's _____. "I think it's gone
                             PART OF THE BODY

_____," Linda said, pinching her _____ after
   ADJECTIVE   PART OF THE BODY

catching a single whiff. "To my _____ bride," Bob
                                   VERB ENDING IN "ING"

said, raising the sauce high. "I wish I could _____ you all
                                                   VERB

over again!" The moment was cut short. Bob rushed off to (the)

_____ to vomit.
   A PLACE

MAD LIBS® is fun to play with friends, but you can also play it by yourself! To begin with, DO NOT look at the story on the page below. Fill in the blanks on this page with the words called for. Then, using the words you have selected, fill in the blank spaces in the story.

Now you've created your own hilarious MAD LIBS® game!

THE ONES THAT GOT AWAY

PERSON IN ROOM (FEMALE) _____

TYPE OF LIQUID _____

NOUN _____

PART OF THE BODY _____

ANIMAL _____

ADJECTIVE _____

VERB ENDING IN "ING" _____

TYPE OF FOOD _____

NOUN _____

VERB (PAST TENSE) _____

NOUN _____

PERSON IN ROOM (MALE) _____

NOUN _____

OCCUPATION _____

NOUN _____

NOUN _____

NUMBER _____

THE ONES THAT GOT AWAY

A partial list of _____'s star-crossed loves:
<u>PERSON IN ROOM (FEMALE)</u>

Josh: The boy she met while behind the _____ fridge.
<u>TYPE OF LIQUID</u>

She grabbed the _____-Aid off his _____, which
<u>NOUN</u> <u>PART OF THE BODY</u>

covered a/an _____ bite.
<u>ANIMAL</u>

Jairo: A/An _____ dance _____ instructor
<u>ADJECTIVE</u> <u>VERB ENDING IN "ING"</u>

Jonas: The melodica-playing _____ delivery
<u>TYPE OF FOOD</u>

_____
<u>NOUN</u>

Jeff: A ghost the Belchers _____ in the basement of
<u>VERB (PAST TENSE)</u>

their _____
<u>NOUN</u>

_____: A "bad _____" Wagstaff student
<u>PERSON IN ROOM (MALE)</u> <u>NOUN</u>

with his own graffiti tag

Dr. Yap: The Belcher family _____
<u>OCCUPATION</u>

Jimmy Pesto Jr.: The _____ of her life and the
<u>NOUN</u>

_____ of her dreams. She has logged over _____
<u>NOUN</u> <u>NUMBER</u>

fantasy hours with this guy

MAD LIBS® is fun to play with friends, but you can also play it by yourself! To begin with, DO NOT look at the story on the page below. Fill in the blanks on this page with the words called for. Then, using the words you have selected, fill in the blank spaces in the story.

Now you've created your own hilarious MAD LIBS® game!

EVERYTHING MUST GO

A PLACE _____

NOUN _____

ADJECTIVE _____

PLURAL NOUN _____

PLURAL NOUN _____

ADJECTIVE _____

A PLACE _____

CELEBRITY (MALE) _____

NOUN _____

ADVERB _____

ARTICLE OF CLOTHING _____

TYPE OF FOOD _____

NOUN _____

ANIMAL _____

PLURAL NOUN _____

NUMBER _____

ANIMAL _____

EVERYTHING MUST GO

In hopes of de-cluttering their _____, the Belcher family is
                                            A PLACE

having a/an _____ sale! To make it _____, the
                 NOUN   ADJECTIVE

family member whose prized _____ bring in the most
                                  PLURAL NOUN

_____ will decide how the cash gets spent. Bob and Linda
PLURAL NOUN

want a/an _____ refrigerator. Tina wants a family trip to
                ADJECTIVE

(the) _____ in hopes of meeting _____.
          A PLACE   CELEBRITY (MALE)

And Gene insists the restaurant needs a/an _____ and sound
                                            NOUN

system. But the sale doesn't run as _____ as planned. Linda
                                   ADVERB

refuses to sell her wedding _____ to her sister Gayle.
                           ARTICLE OF CLOTHING

Bob gets caught bribing Jimmy _____ Jr. to buy his
                                TYPE OF FOOD

childhood _____ collection. And after Louise knocks over
                 NOUN

Gene's _____ farm, _____ won't come within
             ANIMAL   PLURAL NOUN

_____ feet of the restaurant. "I win!" Louise says. "Finally,
NUMBER

I can buy that guard _____ I've always wanted!"
                         ANIMAL

MAD LIBS® is fun to play with friends, but you can also play it by yourself! To begin with, DO NOT look at the story on the page below. Fill in the blanks on this page with the words called for. Then, using the words you have selected, fill in the blank spaces in the story.

Now you've created your own hilarious MAD LIBS® game!

FRIEND FICTION

NUMBER _____

PERSON IN ROOM (MALE) _____

PART OF THE BODY _____

OCCUPATION _____

ADJECTIVE _____

SAME ADJECTIVE _____

VERB ENDING IN "ING" _____

PART OF THE BODY (PLURAL) _____

ADJECTIVE _____

VERB ENDING IN "ING" _____

VERB (PAST TENSE) _____

ADVERB _____

PART OF THE BODY (PLURAL) _____

EXCLAMATION _____

ADVERB _____

A PLACE _____

FRIEND FICTION

Paris, _____ years ago. Tina and _____
                NUMBER   PERSON IN ROOM (MALE)

walked arm-in-_____ along the water. They passed a/an
                  PART OF THE BODY

_____ playing "What a/an _____ World" on a
   OCCUPATION   ADJECTIVE

violin. "Do you think the world really is _____?" Tina asked
                                            SAME ADJECTIVE

him. The two stopped _____ for a moment. He smiled
                        VERB ENDING IN "ING"

and gazed into her _____. "I think it's _____,"
                      PART OF THE BODY (PLURAL)   ADJECTIVE

he said with a lisp. "Just like you." Tina couldn't believe what

she was _____. Her eyelids fluttered and she
          VERB ENDING IN "ING"

_____ backward! The gentleman leaped forward
   VERB (PAST TENSE)

_____ and gallantly caught her in his _____.
 ADVERB   PART OF THE BODY (PLURAL)

"Tina!" he cried. "My beloved! _____!" They have lived
                                  EXCLAMATION

_____ ever after in (the) _____, ever since. The end.
   ADVERB   A PLACE

MAD LIBS® is fun to play with friends, but you can also play it by yourself! To begin with, DO NOT look at the story on the page below. Fill in the blanks on this page with the words called for. Then, using the words you have selected, fill in the blank spaces in the story.

Now you've created your own hilarious MAD LIBS® game!

BURGER OF THE YEAR

TYPE OF FOOD _____

NOUN _____

PART OF THE BODY _____

LETTER OF THE ALPHABET _____

TYPE OF LIQUID _____

TYPE OF FOOD _____

NUMBER _____

COLOR _____

OCCUPATION _____

ADJECTIVE _____

NOUN _____

VERB (PAST TENSE) _____

NUMBER _____

TYPE OF LIQUID _____

PART OF THE BODY _____

COLOR _____

BURGER OF THE YEAR

In honor of Mr. Fischoeder, judge of the annual _____
TYPE OF FOOD

contest at the _____ Wharf, Bob has created a new
NOUN

masterpiece: The _____-patch Burger! For his submission,
PART OF THE BODY

Bob took two grade-_____ beef patties, brushed them
LETTER OF THE ALPHABET

with a reduction of _____ vinegar, then dredged them in
TYPE OF LIQUID

crushed _____ chips. Bob then broiled the patties in a/an
TYPE OF FOOD

_____-degree oven until they were a crispy golden
NUMBER

_____. With the precision of a/an _____, Bob
COLOR   OCCUPATION

stacked the patties atop a/an _____-dough bun, covered it
ADJECTIVE

all with a fried _____, and then _____
NOUN   VERB (PAST TENSE)

a ribbon of _____ island dressing across it. When he was
NUMBER

done, Bob wiped the _____ from his _____.
TYPE OF LIQUID   PART OF THE BODY

"Aww, Bobby!" Linda cooed. "It looks like a little baby! I can't wait to

see him wear a/an _____ ribbon!"
COLOR